The First Seventeen Years

V

www.trafford.com

North America & International
toll-free: 1 888 232 4444 (USA & Canada)
phone: 250 383 6864 ♦ fax: 812 355 4082

In memory of my abusive loving father for making me Stronger than I knew I was. You will never be forgotten. To the rest of my family all my love.

When the pressures of life become too much
The sky black and dark
When you seek and do not find
Perhaps you're looking for the wrong thing
When you are wronged once and it begins again
Put yourself first and others last
When he beats you touch you
The weakling you once spoke of
You now have become

I get sad and upset
My past will not stay in the past
One day a man I met
This man was not of my kind
He was warm and sincere
And he did not mind
So to my heart he became dear
Yet once again my past
Had to remind me
Of all characters in my family cast
And him I set free

I know I have not been myself lately
I have been someone
I do not really like too much
But believe me when I say
That it's because of someone else
If I have been distant
If I have said things
That made you feel bad
I did not intend to
Please forgive me
I am just going through
A difficult time right now
And sometimes it makes me hurt
The very people
I care about the most
All I can say is that
I am sorry
The last thing I wanted to do
Is hurt someone
Who is as special to me
As you

Now is not the time
It is hard for me
Some days you remind me of another
The way you move
Or a glance from your blue eyes
And I feel as though
This happened yesterday
You say you love me
I want to believe you
Once before another said
"I love you"
I have learned
That those three little words
Affect people in different ways
Three words we all have heard
Their meaning left earlier that day

What is this weight
That lies heavy
On my shoulders
What is it that
Keeps me in a cage of darkness
Could it be
The darkness of life
Could it be
The dawn before day
Could it be a person
A person who watches
Like a hawk waiting
For darkness to fall
So it can attack
What is this
Weight that lies
Heavy on my shoulders

When the pressures of life become too much
The sky is dark and black
When you seek and do not find
Find yourself looking for the wrong thing
When you are wronged once and it begins again
Put yourself first and others last
When he touches you and you cannot stop the blows
The weakling you once spoke of
You have now become.

I get sad and upset
My past will not stay in its place
One day a man I met
This man was not of my kind
He was warm and sincere
He did not mind my past
He only saw my future
So to my heart he became dear
But once again my past
Had to remind me
Of all the characters in my families cast
And I set him free
He violated my personal space
He became dear to my heart
He wanted to go to his place
I had to let him free
This time from my heart

I know I have not been myself lately
I have been someone
I do not really like very much
But believe me when I say
That is simply because of him
If I have been distant
If Ii said things
That made you feel bad
I did not intend to
Please forgive me
I am just going through
A difficult time right now
And sometimes it causes me
To hurt the very people
I care about the most
All I can say is that
I am sorry
The last thing I wanted to do
Is hurt someone
Who is as special to me
As you.

I know you are disappointed
I am as well
Now is not the time
It is too hard for me
Some days you remind me of others
The way you move
Or a glance from your blue eyes
And I feel as though
It happened yesterday
You say you love me
I want to believe you
Once before someone told me
"I love you"
I have learned
That those three little words
Affect people in different ways
Three words we all have heard
Their meaning left earlier that day

What is this weight
That lies heavy
On my shoulders
What is it that
Keeps me in a cage of darkness
Could it be
The darkness of life
Could it be
The dawn before day
Could it be a person
A person who watches
Like a hawk waiting
For darkness to fall
So it can attack
What is this
Weight that lies
Heavy on my shoulders

Now is the time
For dreams and wishes
Now is the time
For all good things
Now is the time
For people in love
Now is the time
For hope and joy
Now is the time

Wandering lost and alone
I am as far away from you
As the sun from me
You are still waiting
I am searching for an answer
Try and understand
Though I try
I cannot fool myself
I have got to keep moving
In order to find myself

Trying to figure out
Where you are
You tried to play the game
And it went too far
You said you would be nobody's fool
You want to know now
Why this game is so cruel
I think this game
Was not meant for you

Blinking bright colors of joy
For every little girl and boy
Give them hope
Give them what they really need
Give them dreams
Make things better than they seem

My knight in shining amour
All my wants and needs
My hopes are in thee
To fill my heart with dreams

Happy Mother's Day to you
May all your wishes soon come true
I would like to say I love you
On this very special day
No other mother would go further
To help me through my daily trials
And help me walk those extra miles
On the 10th of May
On this very special day
The love I feel for you
It is not false it is true

Seek and you shall find
Look hard for what it is
That troubles you
Look through your heart
Not with your eyes
You will find it
So do not despair
All that is necessary is to
Seek and you shall find

We have been to the end of the rainbow
We had our chance at life
It is our time to step down now
And let the children lead the way Cherish what we had
Our reign is over
We can be together
Until the end of time

It was hard for minorities to receive an education
In the beginning there was not a school for Blacks
Schools were considered too well for us
We had to struggle and fight
So we could be able to see the light
It took awhile
We walked several miles
We kept trying with all our might
There was nothing strong enough
Nothing that could last long enough
To keep us from learning
In the end we were like flowers
Learning made us grow
We were held back
But not for long
Finally we united
We have made this world a better place
The great Martin Luther King Jr said
"We shall overcome"
And we did

I have no clue
How anyone could not love you
Then you came along
And found away
Do you have a heart
Even a little smarts
Once I loved you
That I cannot deny
But once is no more
That is why I will not cry
It does not matter now

Nothing to lose
So I write the blues
I gave you my soul
Know I have nothing to hold

A young Black girl
Not made for this worlds pain
Slanted eyes
Filled with tears
Like black mud looks
After a rain
Glasses resting
Laying on my ears
My cheeks no kiss
Has left a stain
Lips drawn up from
The fear of love
In the night my eyes
Shine brighter than a dove
And still before me
Lay several miles

I was made from clay
In just one day
My seventeen years
I have shed many tears
One day my name
Will be associated with fame
I have separated myself from someone dear
This I have done because of fear
From my heart
You will always be apart
I have traveled a weary road
Filled with toil and strife
It is time now to close
This chapter of my life

The last of a dying breed
That ought to die out
They cause trouble
And create problems
They are the drunk drivers
And the serial killers
The thugs and the hoodlums
They make some women's lives miserable
Treat them like dirt
And some women go right along
With the game
Women are fools dummies
When it comes to men
You're in a spell
And cannot tell right from wrong
The worse the treatment
The more you love him

I wish today would go and stay
And yesterday could be here always
I wish the pain would go away
With God's blessing soon it may
I wish the tears would run no more
Let things be as they were before
I wish the sky to always be blue
Never black and gloomy just for you
I wish that you could love me right
And one day soon see the light

In the dark sky
There is no eye
There is not a trace
Not even a raveled lace
I hid
The sin that was committed
As I began falling
I could hear something calling
My heart tells me of your lies
Honesty not in your eyes
Hopefully flying over head
Soon this chapter will be dead
As a bad reminder I will stay
So I can remind you everyday

Birds in the sky
Flying high
The moon in the sky
Bout to die
The blackness of night
Takes away my fight
You have clipped my wings
With one little sting
Once I danced under the sun
I had fun
Once I was young and vibrant
Filled with little girl chants
Once I was a virgin
In a lion's den
Now I cry from my eyes
As the cars pass me by
Now I am old and half dead
The riot act I have been read
Now I am mean
Nothing stays the same
Not even silly little kid games

Here I lay looking around me
For my royal majesty
The hurt in my eyes
Tells of the truth not lies
Will it settle the dust
Why have I been treated so unjust
Your soul has turned cold
My eyes are visibly sad
Your emotions grow bold
The hatred turns me mad
What I do I do in pain
What you do you do in vain